CYNGOR CAERDYDD
CARDIFF COUNCIL
LIBRARY SERVICE

CARDIFF
CAERDYDD

Ar

C

D1434689

Philip

First published 2013 by Kingfisher
an imprint of Macmillan Children's Books
a division of Macmillan Publishers Limited
20 New Wharf Road, London N1 9RR
Basingstoke and Oxford
Associated companies throughout the world
www.panmacmillan.com

Series editor: Polly Goodman
Literacy consultant: Hilary Horton

ISBN: 978-0-7534-3096-5
Copyright © Macmillan Publishers Ltd 2013

9 8 7 6 5 4 3 2 1

1TR/1012/WKT/UG/105MA

A CIP catalogue record for this book is available from the British Library.

Printed in China

Picture credits
The Publisher would like to thank the following for permission to reproduce their material. Every care has
been taken to trace copyright holders. However, if there have been unintentional omissions or failure to trace
copyright holders, we apologize and will, if informed, endeavour to make corrections in any future edition.
(t = top, b = bottom, c = centre, r = right, l = left):
Cover Shutterstock/Gentoo Multimedia; Corbis/Robert van der Hilst; Pages 3t Getty/Martin Hartley;
3ct FLPA/Tui De Roy/Minden; 3c Corbis/Layne Kennedy; 3cb Frank Lane Picture Agency (FLPA)/David
Tipling; 3b FLPA/Jules Cox; 4 KF Archive; 5t KF Archive; 5b Shutterstock/Photodynamic; 6 Corbis/
Alaska Stock; 7 FLPA/Jules Cox; 8 Getty/OSF; 9t Alamy/All Canada Photos; 9b Shutterstock/Gary
Whitton; 10 Corbis/Paul Souders; 11t FLPA/Norbert Wu/Minden; 11b FLPA/Patricio Robles/Minden;
12t Corbis/Glen Bartley/All Canada Photos; 12b Alamy/Steven J. Kazlowski; 13t FLPA/David Tipling;
13b Corbis/ Steven J. Kazlowski; 14 Corbis/Layne Kennedy; 15t ArcticPhoto/Bryan & Cherry Alexander;
15b Corbis/Michel Setbourn; 16 Getty/Imagno; 17t Corbis/Bettman; 17b Getty/Martin Hartley; 18
ArcticPhoto/Bryan & Cherry Alexander; 19t Corbis/Thomas Pickard Photos; 19b Corbis/George
Steinmetz; 20l FLPA/Flip Nicklin/Minden; 20r KF Archive; 21t Shutterstock/nice_pictures; 21b FLPA/
Tui De Roy/Minden; 22 KF Archive; 23t Corbis/Hulton; 23b Corbis/Reuters; 24t Corbis/Galen Rowell; 24b
Corbis/Alfred Wegener Institute/Hans-Christian Woeste; 25 KF Archive; 26 Corbis/George Steinmetz; 27
Corbis/Denis Sinyakov; 28 ArcticPhoto/Bryan & Cherry Alexander; 29 FLPA/ Konrad Wothe/Imagebroker

Contents

The ends of the Earth

If you travel very far to the north or south, you reach lands of ice and snow. These are wild, beautiful places, where it is difficult for humans to survive. These are the polar regions.

The **North Pole** is the most northerly point on Earth. The area around the North Pole is called the Arctic. On maps, the Arctic Circle is drawn around this region. This is an imaginary line that crosses the Arctic Ocean as well as many lands, including parts of Canada, Greenland and Russia.

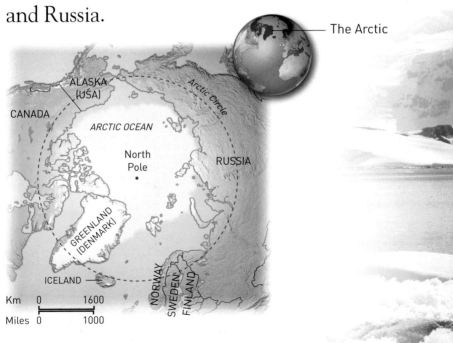

The Arctic

ALASKA
(USA)

Arctic Circle

CANADA

ARCTIC OCEAN

North
Pole

RUSSIA

GREENLAND
(DENMARK)

ICELAND

NORWAY
SWEDEN
FINLAND

Km   0   1600
Miles 0   1000

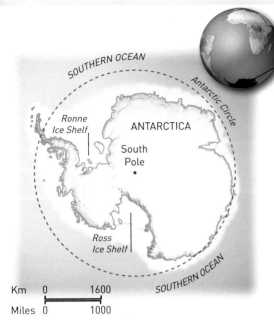

The Antarctic

SOUTHERN OCEAN

Antarctic Circle

Ronne
Ice Shelf

ANTARCTICA

South
Pole

Ross
Ice Shelf

SOUTHERN OCEAN

Km   0   1600
Miles 0   1000

The **South Pole** is the most southerly point on Earth. It lies at the centre of a frozen land called Antarctica. On maps, the Antarctic Circle is drawn around this region. This is an imaginary line that crosses the Southern Ocean.

Penguins live on the ice and rocks of Antarctica.

The big freeze

The polar regions have long, cold winters, when temperatures can drop below −50°C. The short summers can be quite warm in places, but most areas stay cool, with temperatures between −10°C and 10°C.

Around the Poles the air is dry, so new snow does not fall very often. Even so, lots of snow lies on the ice. It is whipped up by strong winds, creating fierce storms called **blizzards**.

It is difficult to see anything in the white-out of an Antarctic blizzard.

Just how cold can it get?

The world's lowest known temperature was recorded in Antarctica, at the Vostok scientific base, on 21 July 1983. It was −89°C!

A group of walruses rest on an Arctic ice floe.

The Arctic and Antarctic are so cold that parts of both regions are covered with ice all year round. During the winter, slabs of floating sea ice, called **ice floes**, form. **Icebergs** break off from the ends of frozen rivers, called **glaciers**, and from big **ice shelves**.

In this book, we will explore both polar regions, travelling first to the Arctic, before heading south to Antarctica.

Lands of the Arctic

The part of the Arctic Ocean closest to the North Pole stays covered in deep ice all year round. Further south, sea ice melts each summer and freezes up again each winter.

The lands around the Arctic Ocean include islands, plains and mountains. They are covered by snow in winter. When the snow melts in the summer, pools of water are left on the surface. This type of landscape is known as **tundra**.

On top of the world

The most northerly patch of land on Earth is an island called Kaffeklubben, in Greenland.

Icy mountains covered by snow drifts lie on the coast of Greenland.

Grasses, mosses and wildflowers grow on the tundra in the summer. No trees can grow here though, because deep down the soil remains frozen all year round.

Further south from the tundra there are great forests of **spruce** and fir trees. Snow falls heavily here in the winter.

Animals in the Arctic Ocean

All sorts of animals live in the Arctic. They have found ways to survive in the bitter cold. The sea is full of tiny plants and animals, called **plankton**. Plankton provides a rich food for many fish, and for the huge whales that cruise Arctic waters. Many seabirds catch the fish.

Cod survival

Arctic cod can survive in colder waters than any other fish. Their bodies produce chemicals that prevent their bodies from freezing, just like the antifreeze that stops cars icing up in winter.

A humpback whale leaps out of the water.

Seals are perfect divers. They mostly feed on fish. Their streamlined bodies help them swim at speed and thick layers of **blubber** keep them warm.

Seals are **mammals**, so they have to come up through holes in the ice to breathe air. There may be a hungry polar bear waiting for them above the ice. This massive bear is the top hunter of the Arctic. It is a powerful swimmer, and hunts on ice floes as well as coastal tundra.

A polar bear catches a seal.

Animals on the tundra

When summer comes and the snow melts, the Arctic tundra comes alive. Wild flowers grow, attracting many insects. These provide a feast for flocks of little birds. Geese migrate from the south to feed on the fresh grasses.

Whimbrels (left) use their long, curved bills to feed on insects, worms and crabs.

Snow geese spend their summers feeding on grasses on the tundra.

Many animals leave the tundra at the start of winter, but some stay on. Many, such as the Arctic fox and its prey, the Arctic hare, have coats that turn white, to **camouflage** them against the snow. The brown feathers of the ptarmigan (say 'tar-mi-gan') become white in winter, too. This bird pecks at buds, seeds and berries.

The Arctic fox turns white in winter.

A long journey

In North America wild reindeer, called caribou, spend the winter in the shelter of the forests. In spring they migrate to the tundra (below). Some herds, numbering hundreds of thousands, travel up to 5,000 kilometres in one year.

Peoples of the Arctic

People settled in the Arctic thousands of years ago. They learned the skills they needed to survive in the harsh **climate**. They wore skins and furs to keep warm, and were expert at fishing and hunting seals.

An Inuit hunter with his team of dogs.

The Inuit people of North America travelled in boats called **kayaks**, or by **dog sled**. They built houses of stone and turf, and shelters made of snow blocks, which we call **igloos**. In the far north of Europe and Asia, peoples such as the Saami and Nenets often made a living from herding reindeer. The animals provided meat, milk, and **hide** to make tents.

These Inuit girls are enjoying a snowmobile ride.

Some people still hunt, fish or herd reindeer, but they may travel by **snowmobile** or plane instead of sleds. Many live in modern villages and shop in modern stores. Others have moved to the cities to find work with the mining and oil companies that are now based in the Arctic.

Arctic fun

Reindeer herders such as the Saami and the Nenets like to hold spring festivals. These may include reindeer racing, reindeer lassoing competitions and snowmobile races.

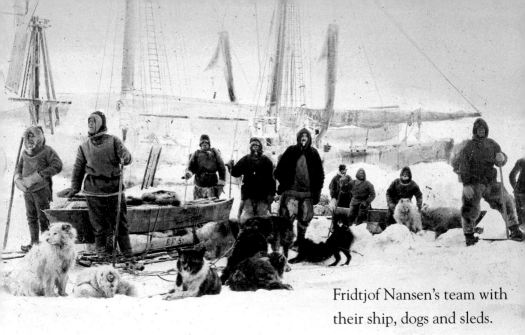
Fridtjof Nansen's team with their ship, dogs and sleds.

Arctic explorers

The first known people to explore the Arctic were the **Vikings**, who settled in Iceland and southern Greenland over a thousand years ago. Hundreds of years later, different explorers tried to reach the North Pole.

In the 1890s, a Norwegian explorer, called Fridtjof Nansen, let his ship, the *Fram*, drift into the pack ice. Then he and another member of the crew tried to reach the North Pole on skis, but the drifting ice made their journey impossible. They eventually got back home three years after setting out.

Robert Peary was a brave Arctic explorer who tried to reach the North Pole on three separate expeditions.

In 1908 and 1909, two Americans called Frederick Cook and Robert Peary each claimed to have reached the North Pole. Since then explorers have reached the North Pole using snowmobiles, dog sleds and skis.

Radio and satellite contact have made Arctic exploration safer, but it is still exhausting and dangerous.

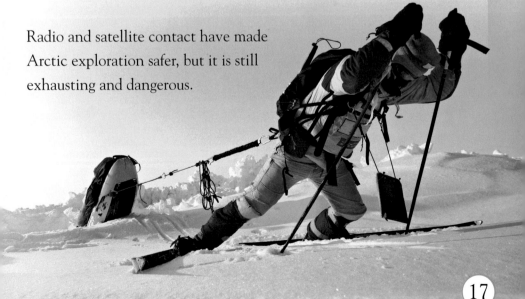

South to Antarctica

On the other side of the world from the Arctic, Antarctica is a **continent** almost twice the size of Australia. It is made up of a solid mass of land and a number of islands.

Almost all of Antarctica is buried under one vast sheet of ice. On average this is about 2 kilometres thick, but in places it can be twice that much. It makes up 90 per cent of all the ice – and over 60 per cent of all the fresh water – on our planet.

Antarctica's plains of ice form a polar desert, crossed by a jagged mountain range.

Glaciers extend out to sea, forming ice shelves along the coast.

In contrast to the Arctic, tundra only forms a tiny part of Antarctica. Very few plants can survive there other than mosses and lichens.

Ice and fire

Mount Erebus, on Ross Island, is an active volcano that is 3,794 metres high. It belches out hot gases and lava. The heat creates strange caves and smoking towers in the ice.

Animals in the Antarctic

Few animals can survive in Antarctica. Inland, the thick ice and lack of plants mean that there is no food. Life is only possible around the coasts and ice shelves.

As in the Arctic, the oceans are a rich source of food. In the sea, tiny, shrimp-like animals called krill eat plankton. The blue whale, the biggest animal on Earth, gulps down tonnes of krill every day.

Krill

Two blue whales open their mouths to gulp down krill.

Another giant of the Southern Ocean is the colossal squid, which can grow to be 14 metres long. Weddell seals live on the ice shelf and feed on fish, squid and krill.

Pole to pole

A small bird called the Arctic tern **migrates** between the Arctic and Antarctic each year. It flies a total of about 71,000 kilometres, the longest animal journey made on Earth.

Five **species** of penguins live in Antarctica. These birds cannot fly, but they are speedy swimmers. Seabirds such as the great skua steal penguin eggs and attack their chicks. Other enemies of penguins include killer whales and a fierce hunter called the leopard seal.

Emperor penguins come ashore to breed, gathering in large groups called colonies.

Antarctic explorers

Russian, British and American sailors first saw the shores of Antarctica in the 1820s. In 1853, an American seal hunter landed there.

In 1910, a Norwegian explorer called Roald Amundsen sailed to Antarctica in Fridtjof Nansen's old ship, the *Fram*. Fifty-seven days after leaving the Antarctic coast, Amundsen's expedition finally reached the South Pole on 14 December 1911.

Amundsen's team used dog sleds and skis to travel quickly over snow and glacier ice.

Scott's expedition arrived in Antarctica in 1911. Scott wrote in his diary: 'Great God! This is an awful place!'

A British expedition led by Robert Falcon Scott arrived at the South Pole after the Norwegians, in January 1912. Scott was disappointed not to have arrived first. On the return journey there were terrible blizzards. All the British explorers died of cold and hunger.

Scott's hut

The hut used by Scott's 1910–1911 expedition still stands in the Antarctic. The cold climate has preserved some of the food and stores as if they had been in a freezer for over 100 years!

Today, Antarctic expeditions have better equipment and support, and even tourists visit Antarctica. Ships cruise the Antarctic coast during the southern summer.

Ice stations

No-one has ever made a permanent home in Antarctica because of the harsh conditions, but scientists stay at the **research stations** there.

International flags surround the marker post at the South Pole.

The mainland of Antarctica does not belong to any one nation, and there are strict limits on who can visit and what they can do. Thirty countries have built research stations there. These ice stations are designed to survive extreme cold and winds of up to 300 kilometres per hour.

This German research station, called Neumayer III, opened in 2009.

Scientists in Antarctica study the weather, because the polar regions affect the climate of the whole world. They study the air, which is the least **polluted** on our planet. They measure the thickness of the ice sheet and the area of the ice shelf. They study the rocks, the plants and the coastal animals.

Scientists use satellite signals from space to check their exact position.

Changing climate

Scientists studying ice and weather in the polar regions warn us that the climate there is changing. Ice sheets are becoming thinner, and the sea ice is melting. These changes are happening very quickly.

Climate clues

The Antarctic ice holds all sorts of useful information. If scientists drill out ice from 3,700 metres of ice sheet, they can find out what the climate has been like over the last 500,000 years!

The mining city of Norilsk, in the Russian Arctic,
is one of the most polluted places in the world.

The climate is getting warmer in the rest of the
world, too. Many scientists blame it on humans,
because we burn up fuel and take part in other
activities that give out harmful gases. The gases
gather in a layer around the Earth, trapping heat
and making the climate warmer.

The polar climate is important to us all. It affects
the Earth's winds, ocean currents and sea levels.
A big melt could cause low-lying islands and
coasts to be flooded all around the world.

Fishing and hunting by the Inuit depend on the survival of Arctic wildlife.

The future

The Arctic and Antarctic have changed greatly in the last 100 years. If the climate keeps getting warmer, there will be even bigger changes for the people and wildlife who live there. If the ice keeps melting on the land and oceans, polar bears, walruses and penguins will struggle to survive.

If the sea ice keeps melting, more and more ships will be able to pass through the Arctic Ocean. Mining and oil companies want to move into new areas of the Arctic, to extract valuable minerals and oil. Antarctica also has many minerals, but since 1961 the world's nations have agreed to keep it as a special international **refuge**.

Boats beat the ice

For hundreds of years, explorers tried to find sailing routes around the edges of the Arctic Ocean. They were always beaten by the ice and many lost their lives. But in 2010 there was so little sea ice that two boats managed to complete the whole voyage.

People in every part of the world need to do all they can to slow down climate change. We can all make a difference, just by using less fuel and power, or by reusing everyday goods. The Arctic and Antarctic are too precious to destroy.

Glossary

blizzard Wind that carries snow.

blubber A layer of fat that protects whales and seals from the cold.

camouflage Patterns or colourings that make an animal blend in with its surroundings.

climate The typical weather conditions over a long period.

continent One of the world's seven largest masses of land.

dog sled A platform on runners, pulled across snow or ice by dogs.

glacier A deep, frozen river, which moves very slowly.

hide Animal skin used for making clothes or tents.

ice floe A sheet of ice floating in a sea or river.

ice shelf A wide ledge of ice formed where a glacier or ice cap meets the ocean.

iceberg A large block of ice that has broken off from a glacier or ice shelf.

igloo A round shelter made from blocks of frozen snow, used by Inuit hunters.

kayak A canoe-like boat paddled by Inuit hunters.

mammal An animal that drinks its mother's milk when young.

migrate To travel long distances in search of places to breed or feed.

North Pole The most northerly point on the planet.

plankton Tiny plants and animals that float in the ocean.

polluted Poisoned or made dirty with waste.

refuge A place that is protected from danger.

research station A base for scientific research.

snowmobile A motor vehicle used for crossing ice or snow.

South Pole The most southerly point on the planet.

species A group of animals or plants that can breed together.

spruce A type of evergreen tree that has leaves like needles.

tundra An open region of the Arctic or Antarctic with very few trees. Tundra is frozen in the winter, but the soil on the surface melts in the summer.

Vikings Seafaring people who lived in Denmark, Sweden and Norway from the 700s to around the 1000s CE.

Index